*Words
for Someone Else's Music*

Also by Wallace Caminsky:
All Fathers Are Giants

Words
for Someone Else's Music

Wallace Caminsky

NEW ALEXANDRIA PRESS
LIVONIA

Published by New Alexandria Press
PO Box 530516
Livonia, Michigan 48153
www.newalexandriapress.com

The following poems first appeared in *All Fathers Are Giants*, Copyright
©2008 by Wallace Caminsky: Winter is a Heavy Thing, I'm Around Here
Someplace, Consider How It Was, Let The Auto Club, Something
Green, Cultural Impotence, Gone, Where, Now, The Pain of Now,
Bureaucracy, New Mother, Up North, For Jeff aged almost three, Dinner
Time, A Detroit Fog, Jeff, The Brothers, Standards and Values, Dying,
The Block, The Chameleon is a Small Lizard, Don't Tell Me About
Poems, Jack!, Tomorrow's Monday, The Man Died, September 8, 1957,
John: 11:22:63, An Ode to Exxon and Lost Children, Getting Old, Being
Eighty-Five.

ISBN-10 1-60916-016-3
ISBN-13: 978-1-60915-016-7

Copyright ©2012 by Wallace Caminsky

Cover design by Jeffrey Caminsky.

Printed in the United States of America

10 9 8 7 6 5 4 3 2

For Alice, and a life well-loved....

Contents

*Words
for Someone Else's Music*

Words

Words are spoken music.
Their rhythms soothe or stir the senses.
Like an anthem they can rouse
   the fervor of a people
   or ease the plan of a loss.

Some words roar with indignation.
Others whisper tenderly of love.
They can describe moments that never die
Or visions that vibrate with beauty.
Frost—Cummings—Whitman are musicians
   who play with the alphabet
   to strum magical sounds.

I'm Around Here Someplace—

Oftentimes lately, I am lost
And the world becomes an Empty Word
Where nothing sings, where nothing grows.

Such content then—like to a big-lipped
Bruised child—to find your arms.

Roads

Roads are threads
that stitch a country together
But it was always a work in progress,
   Working in fits and starts
   With no flow, no master plan.

Some of the roads had
   Haphazardly, almost accidentally
   Achieved a connection
   That enriched the whole.
Others, fractured and bloodied
   The area they passed through,
   Filling it with hate and fear
   And loathing,
Threatening to shred
   A work conceived in liberty.

But magically, at critical junctions
   A road would make the turn
   that would illuminate an age:
at a log cabin in the woods,
at a mansion overlooking a river,
or at a shrine where
a dream was visualized.

Fading to Light

Sun still shines or hides its light as
it will. We write no music.

HE: No, NO, NO...It's not that way. The
    World is vibrant and feels our hearts.
    And Spring can fall from blustering skies.

SHE: Stop trying to act like Byron!
    When it's cold we freeze!

STAR: (laughing nervously) I beg your pardon.

SHE: Who are you?

HE: Yeah, who are you to break in like that?

STAR: I'm sorry but I have to say
    That the young man is right. All the lights of
    Day and night are pledged to ebbing moods
    Of dreamy loves. He's right. He sees the
    Telescoping Time, the shifting seasons;
    Spring born green from gray December, the
    Chimes that ring.

SHE: But . . . .

STAR: Say nothing, the sun rises, kiss
    quickly before I'm gone.

SHE: Must you encourage him? He sounds too much
  Like Shelley now.

HE: You said Byron before.

STAR: Be still, the sun is rising.

The Porch

A wide sloping meadow
  flows from the porch
The view is loud
  with living, growing
Things that tickle
  the feet when comfortably
Walking to the shed
  where the slope ends.

A tree house grows
  by a thick forest
Edging into a swampy pond,
  a hiding place
For secret lives
  That stir when the light dims.

With a porch
  there should be rain,
A swing, a little reason
  to run through the rain.
The forest pulses
  with the laughter
That brightens the day
  and the lives that hear it.

Birthdays

Birthdays . . .
Are really punctuation marks . . .
Periods . . . mostly.
Sometimes an exclamation point . . .
  "Happy New Year!"

But mostly periods . . .
Citing the end of a thought
  which is the year.

Each year is a different thought.
Each thought is a complex
  of different visions . . .
    some happy, some sad.

Through all the visions
One should always sustain you . . .
There is always love
That endures more deeply
After each period.

All Fathers Are Giants

All fathers are giants.
Violent as all giants are,
they tingle with the monumental
whether the monumental be something
Fearful as restitution,
Or exciting as the bleachers,
They tingle.
When the tingle is gone,
Their sons are fathers.

New Mother

My bride is a little girl.
Sweet pouting mouth.
My bride so soft, so small,
Such large wonder in her eyes.

A big boy, Jeff crawls after her.
Demanding.
Smiling the sweetly selfish smile of babies.
My bride loves him
Works for him
And me.

And she cries, sometimes.
It's hard being bride and little girl all at the same time.

Jeff

Our Jeff has seen three Summers come and go
   (but only two Falls and Springs)
And he has grown deeply wise and solemn
And intolerant of any adult nonsense
   (it doesn't pay, he says).
Like tonight—
   We were studying a big white moon,
   Jeff and I were,
   From his bedroom window
and watched how it dived (like a fish, he said)
behind the ragged clouds it met
and how it changed the backyard into something else,
something else that we didn't have when we bought the
house
   (I asked him, "What?" and he answered, "Something!"
and I could see that he was right)

Then he jumped
   (I thought, in my grown-up ignorance that he had
      fallen but he said that he had jumped).
And landed sitting on the floor.
   He would jump to the moon, he announced.
To the moon, he repeated getting up.
And I smiled, that I'm-older-than-you smile, and it made
Jeff mad.
Sooo—

   :in his blue pajamas that were rolled up because he
   tripped over them sometime:

He scrouched way way down
clenched his fists
made a terrible hard face
and jumped!
And when he landed
he laughed
    Right out loud.
"You see? I told you. Didn't I now?"

I looked around in surprise
and, By George, as always
He was right.

The Block

If there's a was
there must be a been
which means there could be a be

Once, remember, living song
the eyes read poems too fast for hand to hold
   Rain hanging, full-bellied from green
   Budding April spilling miniature Niles
   In the mud and the wondrous deltas at the edge

   Of porous sidewalks
   The splash of it was like the diamonds of cymbals
   The spark of water

Even later with Autumn
The faraway straight smoke
Long hellos from woods steeped in gold and reverence
Shaking off leaves like dogs:
Melody coming then fading too quicky
   When you forget

Even later
With the hard cosmetic of Winter
And haloed street lamps
The fog of breathing

All these made dumb the world
Needed puzzling furrows
And poses and words that trembled and lit fires

It's 10:30 and tomorrow
Spring must be met
Or Winter comes to be seen again
And stays too long.

Dinner Time

Jeffy jiggles.
Chrissy wiggles.
Mother purses.
Father curses.

"Eat your string beans while they're hot!"

Chrissy spills.
Jeffy shrills.
Mother moans.
Father groans.

"The wall's a greasy polygot!"

Jeffy incites.
Chrissy indicts.
Father belches.
Mother squelches.

"Stop that squabbling on the spot!"

Chrissy sulks.
Jeffy skulks.
Mother entreats.
Father bleats.

"No desert unless you squat!"

Jeffy jiggles.
Chrissy wiggles.
Parents done.
Kids have won.

"Well call when our nerves unknot."

"Have you ever considered," she says to him,
"That you and I are just an interim?"

Bebop

Crazy crazy crazy
swing that crazy crazy
Twitch
that twitching limb that twitch
and itch of rubbing branch of rubbing
Limb

Always the itch, always the beginning
The end
The itch
  The middle muddled
Muddy muddled middle
where the straining press
against beginning and end cancel out zeroes
And the whoosh of a collapsing
Vacuum sounds like the echoing
sea heard in Midwest sea shells

That crazy rocking swinging zero

The itch is big getting smaller
but worse when smaller because in the quiet
It's there
Tiny tinytiny sniggering
Itch

Crazy crazy neck-corded running with the itch
The twitch

To remember yourself to put yourself
Down—right here—
And become eyes big bigger bigger zeroes for eyes
Hungry sucking eyes
too much mouth all mouth

Never still
Big-lipped

Businessman's lunch for the windsor knots, button collar
and shortpartedhair duck-footed stride and
Teethteethteeth
    Spinning into the next hundred years
with chopped sirloin french fries and iced tea

Tumbling into blasted wreck of a desert
twitching black limbs buried
By sand burning burning with sales
Figures for April into Black
crumbly ashy fists

One reason why I
    Should work here?
    Insurance retirement pay challenge
    future potential young openings
    aggressive hot shots
    How about hold feeling
    How love like belong
    How makes go create construct build
    establish fight die

There's nothing about love in the application blank,
Mister

Last place I worked was all right
Let Me Tell You Brother
Didn't do nothing all day
   Not nothing
Big pay never bothered you and didn't do nothing
Just watched the

Big-titted hip waggling young babes
Tight across the back
hollow right over the ass the cloth throbbed and pulsed
when she walked meat curving calves
On black heels and the crazy crazy
Itch in the eyes—the pouting
loose lipped looked in the cloud eyes

Crazy crazy crazy

How the itch twitch muddles the muddle
   Sex ain't good for business not real thigh
Twitching hot sticky biting
Sex
Not animal god-like tumbling
Sex
not rubbing stiff shuddering
not swearing husty not the naked breasted
Face of sex
not the honest nude
the naive shy the straining brutal

Desex Nature ain't always right
Write on paper make number from it
dance it sing it advertise it in color
But cut out that
Crazy twitching itch

I mean it now
A crazy twitch
   Only no kisses no giggles no games

Zelig

Some people are always spectators, even of their own
lives.
They tend to stand to one side, looking on as their
person
Attempts to engage in life: sex, anger, love, whatever.
They don't need mirrors to read their visage, it's there
before them
Sometimes fascinating them, sometimes repelling them
As they watch themselves change as circumstances change
Or as the cast of characters change.

For Jeff, aged almost three—

Now there are two
where for almost three years you reigned supreme
And the pain of it begins.
 The toys you must share
  Your mother's smiles and kisses
The hurts of occasionally being overlooked.
 Your end as a god.
 Your beginning as a man.
Just remember,
  You were the first to capture our love.
  And its measure will never diminish

Tomorrow's Monday

Sundays die with starts
Of neon flickers, where a breeze
Ruffles a street lamp's shadows.
  Paper
And rope and a roto section
And boys study magazines
In a slow drugstore.
  The traffic light
Repeats itself time and again,
Like the absent prayers of the troubled.
Dust and dust blow through.
  It's the time
Of the thief in the market aisles,
Time of the cat in the emptied lot,
Time of the siren in some other place.
  Across still ball fields,
Under lullaby trees,
Windows cry light,
Antenna fingers sift the air.
  Heels ring sinister,
Glowing cigarettes ominous.
Dogs pass the word from yard to yard:
A walker! A walker!
  Down the grass nibbled pavement,
Under the face brushing fingers
Of old, old trees that little boys leap for.
  Sundays should also die profoundly:
only the very young know
the exciting crack and buckle of sidewalk.

Winter is a Heavy Thing

Winter is a heavy thing
Like too much sleep

The bones ache with Winter
it plays no games—no
Nonsense, please.

Spring is a young harlot
Limpid moist excesses and coy, twinkling
Whispers of green green
Experienced in innocense
The art of pleasing
   A concubine season.

Winter is a heavy thing
yet honest, dependable in its weight, gloom
But honesty isn't something you fall in love with.

September 8, 1957

Dear Jeff and Chris:
I want to talk about your grandpa again.
You will forget him soon.
   And you should.
Your concern is and should be with living
not with death. Death will come in its own good time.

I will forget him too.
Not his face: pictures can always bring it back.
   but what he was and how he was in the round.
I will forget:
   how he sat, how he turned and walked,
   how he spoke, how he laughed;
   the smell, sweat, flesh of him will never come back.

In this letter, I'm hoping to save something of what he
was so that when you read it later (when you learn how)
you will know a little of him,
   and when I read it, I will remember.

He was a remarkable man, my father.
His age was an age of remarkable men.
Just think of this: he and millions like him left their
native land and came to this strange new country to do
something.
   To want to do something is like being hungry
sometimes.
   And trying to do something, they did something.
Starting with as much of nothing as you can have and still

be alive, they made monuments of their lives.
So he was a remarkable man, but he never believed it.
Just as Columbus or Washington or Galileo never
believed they were remarkable men.

   When they thought of themselves, they thought of
themselves as men, growing old and soft, with families
and responsibilities they hadn't particularly sought,
   and saddled with opportunities that
they'd missed,
   and saddled with the sense that somewhere
along the way their lives had taken a turn they
hadn't counted on.

   But fumbling along, tripping, slipping,
Complaining—like my father—they marked and named
their years
And changed, maybe a little bit, what they found when
they came.

But my father always thought of himself as a failure.
His life wasn't complete,
Its end was ragged.

   Everyone's is: you don't get a chance to dot all the i's
and cross all the t's;
Death always comes before you've had time to finish
tying your shoe.

   Come to think of it, everyone fails. It's part of the
curse of being a man.

   I'm wandering.

   About my father now—

What he looked like, you can tell from the pictures in the albums your mother keeps. You can tell from them about the shape of his face, how his eyes looked at you, how round and short he was.

But you couldn't tell how dark he was,
how rough his cheek and chin.

when I was little like you, he used to rub his cheek against mine to make me squeal and giggle because it felt just like sandpaper.

You couldn't tell how big his head was for such a short man.
And with his hairline gone, how his broad rounded forehead made it look even bigger.

You couldn't see much of his profile: the high forehead, the fine nose, the sensitive delicately drawn lips.

I can remember when I was a little boy, maybe 7 or 8, adoring my father's profile.
We were driving somewhere,
my sister and mother were in the
back seat of the model A Ford,
my father and I were up front.
And I couldn't take my eyes off my father, his face etched sharp against
the sky.

I studied him for along time. Remembering now, I think what I learned from that study was that there was a proud man, a fierce angry man, an explosive man.

He never took his eyes off the
road, never showed by any sign that he was aware of my study.
But thinking back, I think he must have known how closely and adoringly I studied him.

And it must have made him happy.

I guess I'm telling more of how I loved him than of him,
but it's harder than I thought.
He loved his native Russia.
The older he got, the closer to Death,
the more he loved it.
You can understand that.
He played there, learned there.
He ran and felt there.
He left his mother there (he never knew when she died).
He buried his father there when he was still a little boy.
He saw his oldest brother killed there
(he and his brother were digging at a hill of rock salt
that had frozen solid through the winter and it collapsed
on top of the brother, and he was dead).
He loved his native Russia.
Everything that had been happy and young,
Strong and full of hope had happened there.

If he'd lived in a different time,
if the country hadn't been racked by a depression when
he was young with a wife and family to worry about.
If.
   It's hard for a man to be noble and strong and proud
when he doesn't know whether he can feed his family.
And then, it kills something in a man when he knows he
can't and has to ask for help.
   Try to imagine how a strong proud man must feel
to have to sit in a kitchen watching his wife doing her
housework, while he sits staring out the window doing
nothing because something's happened to the factory
whistles.
What does he do with his rage?
With his pride?
With his hope?

-27-

Sure, other people went through the same thing.
Sure they did.
But I'm not talking about other people, but my father.
Maybe he was a poet like your father would like to be.
Poets can't live with Economic Truths.

My father never recovered from the depression.
He lost the young sense that he had control over his
destiny.
For the first time, he faced the prospect that things
outside could destroy him.
And something in him that was young and vital
and full of sunrises died.
    And turned into something else
that was old and sour and dark.
That's the way it will always be.
    Men build an image of themselves:
    Everything must fit that image.
    Then one day, there comes a second,
    or a minute,
        or a day that resists the shaping.
    And the image shatters.
    What you are then, depends on what you do with
the pieces.
With my father, your grandfather,
the pieces stayed underfoot until the day he died.

But for me and I hope for you, this:
    A powerful, strong dark brooding man whose angry
love manifested itself in the sweat and effort of his work.
The eye, fierce and hawklike.
The rough touch and rage that was sweeter than the
softest hand,
        the softest whisper.

-28-

The seven-foot tall of him.
The courage of him when Death presented its card.
His faith in his beliefs and principles.
    — whether right or wrong—his faith.
He was a man.
   I was lucky to have him for a father.
I hope (but doubt) that you'll be as lucky.

     All my love, Jeff and Chris.

Consider How It Was

Consider how it was
And how it will be
And
Must.

My father droned heroic poetry from a stage
  when he was young.
He strummed a guitar and sang of Russia
  when he was older.
He trilled a deadly rattle
  when he died.
    Aside from that:
      Was it a nice day? Was it warm?

My wife's uncle Pete squired an American girl
And had his brain knocked loose by some spirited young
boys.
He pursued a mother-image and married her.
He drank a hole in his stomach and it was cut out.
  And he raves for pancakes to fill the void.
    Aside from that:
      Is it a nice bed? Are you resting?

My wife's husband wrote poetry when he was younger.
He drank a little when he was older
and watched TV—late.
He practices rattling now.
    Aside from that:
      Are you healthy? Are you wealthy?

The bleak hours come fast
    When a family dies.
Everything that was dies and becomes remembering.
And nothing is to be.

Let the Auto Club—

Never go anywhere in a car.
Take a bus.
But if you have to go anywhere
Get off the pavement.

Look for dirt roads that have been forgotten
   Make the turn where no arrow points
   Where no miles are indicated
   Where no place is reached.

Woods you'll find: quiet, tangled and dark.
   Houses hiding and ponds that don't need your picnics.

And best of all, after a long stretch of close pressing
woods,
   Best of all, the explosion of a wide flat sweep of farm
field.
   And off to one corner, clean and strong against the sky,
   A white silo, a red barn, a gray house with green
shutters.

Something Green

I want to write something green
   Something light and fragile as a fat willow's earrings
I want to write something naked green
   Like the first grass pushing up through the brown rot of
last year
I want to write something green.

Cultural Impotence

Cramped spaces grow clogged
   With must
   Stir with dampness and
   Shadowing rot

Deep, deep holes collect,
   Smelling of old locks,
   Roiling:
      Ancient sea beasts
      Straining over leathery
      Eggs.

Gone

The place is haunted.
  Spook rustling terrorizes the eye corners
And the shadowed steps echo dust through
    twilight corridors
      The paycheck carries nobody's signature...

There were hands that fingered instruments
    coaxing metallic silvery tunes.
  Grease the smell of burn.
And the slap that turned wheels build build.

Where

The light of it
   Curves someplace
In a straight line
   That comes back.

The warmth of it
   The beat of it
Stays there,
   Someplace.

Unfinished Thing

A short poem
   uses short words
   like love, life, end.

It gives birth to phrases
   like "edge of greeness."

It's dotted with short pronouns
   like I, me, you, we

Sometimes it turns waltish
   and rambles on
   celebrating nature and breathing
   for stanza after stanza

And then . . . just stops
   not knowing where to go next.

Which is where I'm at.

Now

In the absence of knowing
In the lack of becoming
Near the brink of remembering
Near the plunging of predestining
  Is
  A sliver
  Called now.

Given lines and angles
And the cube of creation
Given a formula that moves
And the brassy tickle
Given an itch, a gnaw
Given a flood

The resulting absence
Splits

The Pain of Now

Nothing like the pain of now.
And like the presence of pain makes the nausea on
  autumn
  hello
The texture of things becomes softer
Then
Shining of gold and yet
Flecked with the echo of green cries
And the benign footfalls of awesome giants
Just below the hill, beyond the horizon, past the season.
  But the time and the pain is now.

Bureaucracy

Everything is Big in the U.S. of A. And getting Bigger...
Except, of course, the people and they're getting smaller.
  Bureaucracy....
  No targets for revolt
    no symbols to loathe
    nothing...
    except Bigness and memos and old golf cards...

I said it first!
Do you hear? I really did
We are the passive generation
The listless, the entertained, the aborbers
  —Sponges—
And history is made behind men's backs.

Dying

Got that new Ford today.
  Smooth,
Exciting feel over bumps
Jet smooth quiet
And trees flowing into one another.

Then a squirrel under the wheels
  Smooth
No bump, no sound.
In the mirror he lay still
Then jerked alive
Long bushy tail lashing
Struggling to the curb
To die.

Christ! What a crazy damn
Squirrel.

Up North

You ought to go up North.
   Its thick with trees there.
They boil and bubble into round green hills.
They'll explode someday.
   But no one lives there.
   They live someplace else.

You ought to see that bridge up there.
   A clipper ship leaping free.
The human body arched thin and moist with the work of
love.
It flies from here to there.

But no one lives there either.

Well hell, a rose is a rose,
   A smell is a smell.

The Brothers

Ed wanted a religion based on four letter words.
   Hate and kill and love and kill and others
   Like a shield in innocent savagery.
   Pick the bones and beat the dreams.
   Dance the dance and grin the grin.
   At the kill, at least one smiles a smile.

Herb wanted a system based on pronouns.
   I and me and us and we.
   We needn't because they might.
   We shouldn't because they can.
   An alegra of ME.
   Preach of love.
   It builds armies.

Rupert wanted a government based on God.
   He had Him picked out.
   Rupert.

The Chameleon is a Small Lizard

I am a chameleon
Would you talk of politics?
Look no further!
Satisfaction guaranteed or your money back!
Perhaps religion?
Say Mac! Try the ten-day plan! Return me, no questions
asked, no obligation.
Baseball, football, golf?
Compare with what you've been using and you'll switch!
The Arts?
Before you decide, see me!
Sex?
Friends, you owe it to yourself!
Perversions of Sex?
No money down! No payments!
Gossip? Racial dirt? Petty hates? The movies?
It's Here! It's Me!
I am a chameleon.
   I accept the terms laid down.
   I submit. I need friends.
   I've lost the need for principles
     Or dogma, or values.
   I am a chameleon.

John: 11:22:63

Once upon a long time ago (maybe yesterday)
　　there was a brief shining moment that made the world
young.
The moment passed a long time ago (maybe yesterday)
　　and the world grew bitter with age.

Yesterday (or maybe a long time ago) a new moment
sparkled briefly,
　　a promise flashed like a quick smile and then was
quenched.

And the world grows old and cold and too sad for
bitterness.

Standards and Values

Standards and values
the success of success, the fast buck the new car TV
eighty-five dollar suits
the firm handclasp, the firm chin
the firm steady eye
the laugh the quip the BA
   the right fraternity
   (it wouldn't be fair to the man, really. I don't care
myself
   I'm just thinking of him)
the right neighborhood the right wife the right nurse
Nurse
   All right: like you say
   It's all for the birds, oaty and hot roasting on the
pavement
   and if you look hard enough you'll always find it.
If you forget about looking, even
That's the trouble really how it is
   you forget just looking
   do this like me maybe:
   Find: A Tree,
      A glancing light,
faraway figures,
   deep stretching night
   Find: A Face, haunted,
      Eyes,
         an open window

A shadowed door and muffled voices: something
to step through and close and lock
   something to fling open and someplace
to run for running and to fall for falling.
It's all very well to say: protest
It's all very well to protest: this is what it should be and
not that
It's all very well to say that: things are unbeautiful, unkind,
unjointed.
But let it be someone else

I saw a tree today
   slim and red and dying all alone
   and the air dusty and sharp with the rumour of Winter
   and I saw that tree

That's why I can't say: protest like
Only: me
Looking for anger and targets for scorn blinds the eye
Blinds the heart
But only: me
   And maybe me can well and often
   And maybe hold and give.

Don't Tell Me About Poems, Jack!

We can see Summer turning to go
from our front window
Dust biting into the weeds across the road
Patches of sky showing where
before it had been solid green
And the haze and smoke of Autumn hangs heavy
on the open fields as I leave for work
Every year at this time I listen carefully
   Because some one always calls to me from faraway
   Most of the time I only hear the trailing end of the cry
   the mourning bluenote that finishes
   Somewhere in the smokey haze and dust and rustling
   harvest of leaves someone is reminding me of
   something I'd forgotten
Every year at this time I hear it
But not as near as before
At least nearer than afterward.
Poems don't just spill out
   Beautiful, complete like seven poplars
   on the crest of a hill.
They come hard, coyly uncooperative
   Like a nail that persists in missing the hammer:
It would be better to have done with them.
Don't worry, they said, you'll outgrow it.
Well...
   I'm still waiting
   I've outgrown quite a bit:

My baseball shoes, bubblegum,
The Rover boys, movies
   (Not cowboys)
   And the pleasures of drink (too much)—
But this other thing:
   I read a line of something
   and it strikes tender and hollow
   reverberations and echoes:
And I'm a stranger
Or walking, I look into a face
   Or watch a bird fly
   Or study a stupid puppy sitting in a puddle of water
Most it seems to be red trees, big-bellied and alone
If I could avoid red trees I think I'd be all right

It's about the middle of September
When the red trees come—
—Damn red-headed trees—
The year sighs a long, shuddering sigh
and, all of a sudden, whoosh!
There they are—
—These damn red trees,
Fat, round red trees
   standing like fatlegged little kids,
Quiet
   not asking you to notice
   but hoping you will:
"Do you like me this way?"
"Do you think I look pretty?"
Yes, dammit, yes!
Only leave me alone
I don't want to write poems.

The Man Died

Look at his shoes
  See how they...
Maybe his gloves
  The way they...
Perhaps his hat
  How it...
Or his house and the furniture
  The way it...

It all fit so well, and still remembers.

What's up?
  poking in closets
  pulling out drawers
  turning scraps of paper

What is it, in the garage?
  behind it
  under the peach tree
  beneath the shrubs

This flexed work glove on the basement stair?
  What?
  This glove retains the habit of a hand:
  This son searches like a boy,
  lost, lost.

Getting Old

Lonely is an aged word
If you are loved and loving, you are not alone
The young may agonize over their isolation,
    But they are stealing the sense
    of the widowed, the wifeless.
If you recognize that each day we live is a gift,
    That the now is the ultimate.
    That the now is the end.
    That the now is the now
Then the touch, the act, the gesture
    is an act of love
    and the act of love
    is the ultimate expression of now.

The question of death comes up...
    Now and then
Usually in rooms cloyed with the scent of arrangements,
The tinge of relief, the touch of regret.
Sometimes...
    it comes with the touch of winter, the twinge of
autumn,
    the cry of spring
But most coldly...
    It comes alone
        In a room when the beat of time is strongest
        When the purpose is shadowed...
As long as there is no reason for its coming
It is not noticed
But that's why the question keeps coming up.

An Ode to Exxon and Lost Children

A while ago (maybe yesterday) I saw a
Squirrel commit suicide
It was sitting at the side of the road...
Every once in a while it would alert up on
    it's haunches, front paws pressed together in prayer.
Leaning out to look down the road....

          This was a while ago (maybe yesterday)
When the TV screens were filled with
        —Black slick long-beaked birds trying
                to flutter out of black slick water and dying
        —Otters with simpering silly smiles
                blinking in embarrassment because they
                couldn't do what otters do
        —Acres of floating fish, seals.
It was the season of nausea

After a while (maybe yesterday) a car came down the
road.
The squirrel waited, reached in prayer, until the car
        was a wheel turn away
Then it ran under the front wheel.
There was a red spat
        The tail twitching, then a fur accent on the
pavement

And maybe a while ago (yesterday)
There were pictures of little ones
        wearing chains in urine-soaked beds.

And faces blemished by blue and red
    streaked swells and young eyes staring
    big and puzzled filled with "why?"
And somewhere else fly stricken eyes and
    mouths of surrendering bones, staring, losing the
will to ask
"Why?"

On Being Eighty-Five

I'm eighty-five, you know
That's old, you know
Everything seems used, seems in need of repair
You know
The future is getting shorter,
  The days shorter
Friends become pensive
  Alert for sighs, pains
    You know
The only lightness that comes, you know
Is the squeal of a two-year old's laugh.

Every November

Since that November,
  My world has gone to crap.
It was suddenly old, faltering, uncertain, vulnerable
  Like a person with Alzheimer's.
"Morning in America" Rot.
Night fell in Dallas and the dawn has yet to come.
I'm looking for someone a light touch,
someone with panache,
Someone with an Astaire-like grace—
Someone who makes me feel that I'm someone special,
that I am capable of significant deeds,
  memorable acts,
  incandescent.
My shoulders are rounded, my eyes search the ground to
avoid stumbling.
Roooaar

How Did You Get So Old So Fast?

He's eighty-five
He sits, tapping his cane against his foot
His eyes are lost, in loose aging skin, in a mindless muse
Or are there memories,
   instincts nudging at his consciousness,
Remembering when the eyes were brightly alert,
The legs quick and strong, the lungs powerful bellows?
When he's called back to now by a question
   or a comment,
He responds like a person aroused from sleep
And when an answer is given or a response stated,
He gradually eases back to a warm, hazy dream.

A Letter to Two Sons

A Last letter to you was to commemorate a father
Who had just died.
This letter is to consider your father for whom
a final stanza is in the works.
For him the major events in his life revolved around four
events:
   An Economic Event
   A Military Event
   A Marriage
   And Two Births

His Mother was tiny woman with smiling lips, light
complexion
And a soft gentle voice.
His father was a dark, smouldering man who loved
Shakespeare
And hated the Hearst newspaper
   And the son took after the mother.
He was quiet,withdrawn cautious about relationships
And sensitive to the stance of others.
Living through a Depression was difficult
Where considerations of money, food, the future
Were daily worry and for the son a source of shame and
embarrassment.
As an adult he resisted strongly worrying too much about
money.
The Depression sensitized him to its effects on the
people around:
His father's dark moods and occasional rages,

His mother's grieving worry and frequent escape into the
fantasy of the movies
And for the son—a deepening affection for his father as
he aged and became
Less of a giant.

Then there a war
Millions were involved
Thousands died
But he always felt like a spectator,
Standing off to one side as events swirled around him
 Or affected the course he was on
His biggest adjustment was coming home.
He had left as a fledging man,
Came back an incomplete man
Saddled with uncertainties, questions, unresolved
conflicts—
Particularly as they effected his relationship with his father
(who was the alpha male?)

Marriage is a play of many acts.
It's a comedy, a fantasy, a tragedy,
For some, a bore but not for your father.
For him, it was a romance; it was a wonder
That the one he loved, loved him back
Because there were some who could have had more to
offer.
The first act is full of passion and the single-minded focus
on one another
To the exclusion of anything else except as it affects the
focus on one another.

The second act introduces a set of characters named Jeff
and Chris

With the introduction of the two, the father's vulnerability
Became marked.
He could be hurt through the son's hurt
Their pain could become his pain,
Their uncertainities, anxieties would be added to his.
But given that, given the "what-ifs",
The "maybes", there was the joy, the surprises, the pride
That tempered or negated the apprehensions, the "oh-mys".

Being 85 was significant
Sitting through memorials for departed friends
As sobering, sad
Speculating about "How much longer?" is
understandable but a waste of time.
So your father will relish such time as is available for you
two and his Alice.

If there's time, the next letter will be for grand-children,
great grand-children
And two lovely daughter-in-laws.

As always with love, Your fading Giant

Mook

There was a street named Commor
Someone remembered a little fat boy
walking down the street
    carrying a violin case...
a violin case would stay with him forever.

Another someone remembered him
    as a bridge partner.
He and his partner bid a Grand Slam
and the bid was made...
He jumped in the air roaring in triumph
came down hard on the chair and demolished it.
The next hand another slam was bid and made
    and another chair was destroyed:
Enthusiasm can be destructive.

He played tennis.
Someone remembered when a friend and he
    tried the game for the first time.
A tennis coach ruled over the city courts:
white tennis shirt and shorts, white socks and shoes.
Sportsmanship: no fits of anger,
    no disputes over in or out,
    no questionable language...
The match lasted one hour...
    the language was loud and blue...
    every shot was loudly and profanely disputed
    and the match ended tied at one to one
    because they both wanted a beer.

Someone else remembered his appetite
   for special foods and drinks.
Someone else remembered his love
   for political arguments.
Someone else remembered his special love
   and care for someone special who was
   passing on.
But one someone cherishes a vision passed
   on by another someone of a fat little boy
   walking down the street carrying a violin case.

Another Year's Poem

An anniversary can spur
   the grown of roses
   the sparkle of jewels
   the flow of chocolates
   the flood of greeting cards

But mostly it freshens
   the oneness of two
   and strums
   the strings of time
   sound a visional melody

It's a love song
   it pulses with
   the joy of being
   and summons
   the wonder of what was
   and what is.

What was—
   an unexpected meeting
   that generated a spark
   blessing two lives.

What is—
   a warm gentle
   embrace that
   comforts this year
   and the years after.

Love Story?

I am me
You are she

(You could be he if I were
talking about a son but
that's a possibility I'm not
prepared to deal with)

We could be we
(but you keep ignoring any
of my proposals to do anything)
but since I can't think of another rhyme for me
I'll let this poem be...BE!

Words for Bob

Memorials are somber things,
   tinged with regrets
and darkened by an empty spot.
His life was filled with laughter,
   his face always looked as though
   it was about to break into a grin.

Going to lunch with him was an adventure.
With others, you ended up
   in a bar, a bowling alley, a book store
   but with Bob, it was a hardware store
   or an Army surplus outlet....
Up and down the aisles he would go,
   giving snorts of pleasure when he found
   a tool, a screw, a nail,
   a twisted iron thingamajig he liked.
He would bring the thing to share
   with his companion...
   "Look at this!"
   "What is it?
   "I don't know but it could be useful."

But the most interesting example
   of Bob's inventiveness was when
   he was putting in a brick patio.
He'd laid the cement foundation when a friend
   dropped by the house and found him
   sitting next to a pile of bricks
   his chin in his hand and a frown on his face.

"What's wrong?"
"I'm having trouble."
"What kind?"
"I want to lay the bricks in a random pattern"
The friend picked up a brick and was about to
place it on the foundation
when Bob sprang to his feet shouting,
"No! No! No!"
"What's wrong?"
"You have to have a plan!"
According to the dictionary, random means
haphazard.

This suggests...
If there is an afterlife, Bob is
standing there with St. Peter earnestly
explaining how he could improve the Pearly Gates.

A Detroit Fog

Morning fog in the city
Makes it small and empty and quiet

Trees along Southfield road
— tired ghosts come a long way.

Autumn

Days dwindling down to a precious few
Starting in September
   When trees get dressed for the season
   When the young mourn summer's farewell
   When the old sense the edge of time
   When the darkness comes early
     and the memories grow sharp.
Fall is an honest season: somber
  shadowy like a thoughtful song
  shared with a cherished loved one.

Is Poetry a Young Art?

About the aged...
With days dwindling down
   the poetry becomes dark, somber
   the touch of the muse is heavy, cold.
There is no clarion call,
   No hint of wonder.
The preoccupation is with
   What is the last thing to be noted:
   A face, a tree, a hand, a sound?

With the young, the now
   Is the important thing:
   The surge of now, the stroke of now,
   The caress of now, the wonder of now.

Ode to "Ode" Friends

The speed limit is 65.
The retirement age is 65.

Five minutes after the hour is 65.
Sometimes it's more special:
   like a home run record.

Or even more special,

Like the years spent with
   someone unique:

Through wars, weddings, recessions,
childbirth, retirements.

The love remains
   as fresh as it was 65 years ago.

But remember, the speed limit
   has now gone up to 75!

Birthday Wish

The happy birthday wish
is for more than the celebrant
who blows out the candles

It's for the ones who shared
the year, including the joys
the sorrows, the losses

But every day is special
when it dawns
with the specialness of you.

Of You I Sing

The wonder of Birth:
   the connection, construction, continuity
Of a life from a shadowy past named Lucy
To a throbbing Present.

The fated survival
   of the distant breaths
   that lead to the exciting now.

How did it happen
   that all the "what ifs"
   were weathered and the one of You
   started towards me?

The wonder of this birthday
   is that it continues
   the warm touch of two
   coming a long time together.

There is a lovesong here.
Its notes are quiet,
its tempo measured
but its melody is treasured.

Another Step

This is another
step toward
our promise of
forever.

The wonder of
the face before me
the kiss that
cements our lives.

All of it
fills each year
with a love that
will never die.

I Am Now

I am now as I was
in the beginning
touched by a voice
that seemed designed
to recite poetry
at a dance where strangers
used an embracing dance
to begin a voyage of forever
where each day ended with a kiss.

It's the Day

One more day to celebrate
One more month to count
One more year to tuck away.

Part of a growing treasure of memories —
    dances, trips
    births,
    lovemaking
    friends
which brighten the days
        months
            years
and eases the pain
of what might come

but you will always have
all my love.

Are You Surprised?

The day came
and we were there,
eyeing one another
and enjoying the view.

Does the day come
earlier each year?
And the question of
how many more
makes each one precious,
since it's shared
with the one
who was part of forever.

Forever can be
a year, a month
a day
or it can be the
moment of Darkness
which follows
a farewell sigh and a kiss

and the kiss is part
of forever.

Where Have They Gone?

Once our scene was filled with faces
That shone with the vision of Tomorrow

Friends became friends with a glance
a word, a smile

The Play of Life
was set to music
celebrating being there
with a someone
who was someone.

Few words were needed
to convey a belief
a feeling, a truth

There was a glow
that was a taste of forever
and a place for many

It lasted until spaces
started to appear
and the sound of goodbyes
blended with choking sobs.

Mirror, Mirror on the Wall

There's a twinge in the glass
and an uneasy glance back
to see what was.

The question of what is trips
over sentences, periods, and dates.

There is no glow or growth.
   No wonder

Anticipation is shadowy
and the look is foreign to what was.

There's another face,
   grating with uncertain eyes
   but with a smile that brightens a room.
And the look that retains the magic
   that strummed the heart
   and stokes the love
   that lasts forever
   with the reflection
   that echoes the vision that was.

Windows

Our picture window
   frames the outside world
from limpid buds growing
   to adult green
   to aging gold.

It frames a life
   from children at play
   or waiting for a school bus
   to vans loading for a move
   to elders walking to keep alive
   or a hearse taking delivery
   of a being grown tired of being.

The back window encloses a life:
   the triumphs
   sorrows
   joys
   surprises
Perennials that mark the passage
and quality of time
spent with a loved one.

After multiple years
the sight grows misty,
the stride tentative
the breath labored
but the love stays
healthy and growing.

Are You Ready?

Death is an inconvenient and inconsiderate caller
barging in without knocking
at awkward moments:
in the middle of a back swing,
a speech, an embrace.
It rarely comes when a duty is fulfilled,
an apology is solicited or offered,
the warmth of love is sparked.

But there are steps that can be taken,
especially with the last—
Tell her you love her as you kiss her goodnight
in case you're not there in the morning.

Steps

A beginning is the start of an end.
The start of many ends can introduce beginnings.

One may be the start of a life with many beginnings:
   A breath, a cry, a smile,
   and ultimately
The most significant beginnings—
   steps toward forever
   like the kindergarten step,
   the thinking step, the wonder step.

And the growing creative steps
that illuminate a life
and sets a path
with a host of beginnings
   with new horizons
   new significant others.

But eventually
there is one step
edging toward the site
of farewell
to one
taking
the final
step.

Go Gentle

A farewell can be voiced
or sung to the beat
of a fading heart.
It can soothe the sobs,
inspire a saga
or paint a memory.
Sometimes it's the last word
before a journey leading
to a shadowy shore.
It can be a nod of thanks
for the end of pain or grief.
Whatever it is
it's part of the rhythm of life
from the squawls of birth
to the rattle of death.
But what of the last view?
With the ultimate farewell
there's the wonder
of what the final awareness
should be—
a smile bright with sunshine
a laugh filled with music
maybe the sight of a tree
kissed by fall colors
or maybe an embrace
before the curtains are drawn.

About the Author

WALLACE CAMINSKY was born in 1922, the first-born son of immigrant parents. After struggling through the Depression and World War II, where he served in the South Pacific, he finished college in 1947, graduating with a degree in English from Wayne State University, and was married the following year, soon to start a family of his own. Working for one of the Big Three automotive companies in Detroit, he wrote intermittently for the next twenty years, before embarking on a second career as a lawyer. He went to law school in the 1960s, and became an administrative law judge in 1975, serving in that position until his retirement in 1987. Always a voracious reader, his tastes in literature range from the short stories of James Joyce and P.G. Wodehouse to the novels of Charles Dickens, and the epic classics of Tolstoy...as well as the comedy of Monty Python. *Words for Someone Else's Music* is his second book.